# Preschool Activities for Family Child Care

# Preschool Activities for Family Child Care

Suzanne Gainsley and Julie Hoelscher

HIGHSCOPE PRESS®

Ypsilanti, Michigan

Published by
**HighScope® Press**
A division of the
HighScope Educational Research Foundation
600 North River Street
Ypsilanti, Michigan 48198-2898
734.485.2000, FAX 734.485.0704
Orders: 800.40.PRESS; Fax: 800.442.4FAX; www.highscope.org
E-mail: *press@highscope.org*

Copyright © 2010 by HighScope Educational Research Foundation. All rights reserved. Except as permitted under the Copyright Act of 1976, no part of this book may be reproduced or distributed in any form or by any means, electronic or mechanical, including photocopy, recording, or any information storage-and-retrieval system, without prior written permission from the publisher. The name "HighScope" and its corporate logos are registered trademarks and service marks of the HighScope Foundation.

*Editor:* Marcella Fecteau Weiner
*Cover design, text design, production:* Judy Seling
*Illustrations:* Jane DeLancey; Judy Seling (p. 24); Noah Weiner (p. 55)
*Photography:*
Bob Foran: 10, 29
Gregory Fox: 36, 53, 57
HighScope Staff: 5, 12, 15, 19, 21, 27, 39, 66, 69, 71
Peter de Ruiter: 30

**Library of Congress Cataloging-in-Publication Data**
Gainsley, Suzanne, 1964-
　Preschool activities for family child care / Suzanne Gainsley and Julie Hoelscher.
　　p. cm.
　ISBN 978-1-57379-565-4 (soft cover)
　1. Family day care. 2. Early childhood education. 3. Early childhood education--Parent participation. I. Hoelscher, Julie, 1949- II. Title.
　HQ778.5.G35 2010
　649'.5--dc22
　　　　　　　　　　　　2010017003

Printed in the United States of America
10 9 8 7 6 5 4 3 2 1

# Contents

**Acknowledgments  vii**

**How to Use This Book  1**
How to Support Children's Development  2
What's in Each Activity  3

**Approaches to Learning  7**
1. Helping During Child Care  8
2. Choosing Balls  9
3. Planting Flowers  11
4. Daily Routine Booklet  14

**Social and Emotional Development  17**
5. Mirror, Mirror  18
6. Child Care Photos  20
7. Follow the Leader  22
8. Homemade Toothpaste  23

**Physical Development and Health  25**
9. Ribbon Dancing  26
10. Batting Balloons  27
11. Animal Moves  28
12. Following the String  30

**Language, Literacy, and Communication  31**
13. Rhyming Objects  32
14. Alliteration I Spy  33
15. Sounds, Sounds, Sounds  34
16. Making Connections  35
17. Animal Cubes  37
18. Story Bag  38
19. Hopscotch With Letter Links  39
20. Wordless Picture Books  40

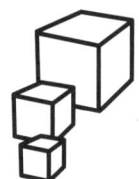

## Mathematics 41
21. Graphing Favorite Fruits 42
22. Ten in the Bed 44
23. Looking for Numbers 45
24. Picture Puzzles 46
25. Play Dough and Marbles 47
26. Measuring by Leaps and Bounds 48
27. Shape Hunt 49

## Creative Arts 51
28. Painting With Watercolors 52
29. Drawing With Crayons 54
30. Art Appreciation 56
31. Texture Collage 58

## Science and Technology 59
32. It's in the Bag 60
33. Magnets 61
34. Listening to Shakers 62
35. Soapy Suds 63
36. Using Timers 64
37. Noticing Changes in Nature 65

## Social Studies 67
38. Going on a Picnic 68
39. Singing Songs 69
40. Babysitting 70

# Acknowledgments

We are appreciative for the opportunity to collaborate and learn from each other. We would like to acknowledge Marcella Fecteau Weiner, our editor, whose keen eye for details makes this a better publication. We would also like to thank Beth Marshall, who initiated this project, and Ann Epstein, to whom we rely on for writing support. Finally, thanks go to Shannon Lockhart, Polly Neill, Kay Rush, and Emily Thompson, our colleagues in the Early Childhood Department who are always available to offer good counsel, resources, and an optimistic vision.

# How to Use This Book

This book provides you — the family child care provider — with activities that will help you support the development of children between the ages of 2½ and 5 throughout your day.

Each activity in this book engages children in active experiences, explains what children are learning in the activity and why it is important for their development, and offers follow-up ideas. This guide also shares how-to guides and recipes for making commonly used preschool materials as well as activities to send home to help parents support children's play and learning.

Each activity in this book focuses on one of eight curriculum content areas that provide children with experiences that support all parts of their learning and development. These content areas include:

Approaches to Learning

Social and Emotional Development

 Physical Development and Health

 Language, Literacy, and Communication

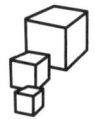 Mathematics

 Creative Arts

 Science and Technology

 Social Studies

# How to Support Children's Development

Children discover and make sense of their world through play. Children tell us a great deal about what they can do, what they know, and what they are interested in during play. They learn best through active involvement with materials, ideas, events, and people. Our role, therefore, is to be thoughtful in our interactions with children as we encourage and support their development. If we observe and understand what children are communicating and learning through their play, we are better able to support their development.

Here are some ideas for you to think about as you use the activities to support children's play and conversation:

- *Join children in their play.* Get on the floor with children, join them at a table or at the easel, play games with them — become engaged in what they are doing!

- *Imitate what the children are doing; that is, play with the same materials in the same way as the children.* For example, at a family child care home, Emma took her portion of play dough that had marbles hidden inside. She squeezed the dough with both hands. The adult also squeezed the dough with both hands.

> During **active learning** children construct knowledge through their direct experiences with materials, ideas, events, and people.

- *Make observations and comments about what you see the children doing.* While watching Emma squeeze the play dough with the marbles hidden inside, the adult commented, "It looks like you have lots of marbles in your dough." Emma responded, "Yeah, and I am going to pick them out and line 'em up."

- *Ask open-ended questions, but ask them sparingly.* Open-ended questions encourage children to talk more, because these types of questions cannot be answered by a simple "yes" or "no." At a family child care home, the adult laid out the puzzle pieces and asked Nathan, "What do you think this puzzle picture might be?" Nathan responded, "I think it's a bear because…look…it's furry." Rather than asking more questions about why Nathan though it looked furry, the adult waited until he completed the puzzle and commented, "It looks like you were right; it is a big, grizzly bear." Questions can help get a conversation going, but it is more important not to inundate a child with questions so that he or she feels overwhelmed.

- *Follow the children's pace and interests.* Belinda was measuring the number of giant steps to the garage at her caregiver's home. She then turned around at the garage door and decided to make "tiptoe" steps to the sidewalk. The adult followed Belinda by making tiptoe steps to the sidewalk (Epstein, 2007).

## What's in Each Activity

Each activity contains the following elements:

- **Activity Title and Content Area Icon:** At the beginning of each activity, you will see an icon representing the primary content area the activity supports.

- **Content Areas:** If the activity involves several content areas, the primary content area is listed first.

- **Why This Is Important:** This section describes what children are learning in the activity and why this is important to their development. You can also share this information with parents to help them relate their children's play to learning outcomes.

- **Materials:** Each activity includes a list of materials to have on hand before the activity takes place. The materials needed are usually available in most homes or are simple to make. Once familiar with how the activities support active learning in each content area, you may find it easy to substitute alternative materials and activities as well as adapt the activities for children in your home who are younger or older.

- **Beginning, Middle, and End:** Each activity is outlined with a beginning, middle, and ending and is based on the principles of *active learning*.

- **Follow-up Activities:** This part offers ideas on what to do on days following the activity to continue the children's learning in a particular content area.

- **Activity to Send Home:** These are included in some of the activities and offer parents ideas on how to extend the children's play and learning at home.

Before using one of these activities, be sure to read through the activity several times and make sure you have all the necessary materials.

> ### Parts of an Activity
> - The **beginning** of the activity encourages children and adults to start the activity, without waiting.
> - Once the children begin working, the **middle** of the activity unfolds, with the adults paying attention to the children's actions and ideas. Children will often use the materials in ways that you might not expect. For example, an adult gave a group of children index cards and different colored buttons at her family child care home. One child sorted the buttons by color, another child counted how many buttons she could put on the index card, and another child decided that the index card was a canoe and the buttons were people who were floating down the Au Sable River!
> - The **end** of the activity gives children closure. Adults give children some control of the closure by asking the children to help clean up the activity and/ or find a spot to display a new work of art.

We hope that you will use these activities in your family child care home to foster your children's development in these eight content areas. In addition, we hope that these activities help you develop as an intentional teacher.

*To support children's play, adults can join them on the floor and make observations about what they see the children doing.*

## Reference

Epstein, A. S. (2007). *Essentials of active learning in preschool: Getting to know the HighScope Curriculum.* Ypsilanti, MI: HighScope Press.

# Approaches to Learning

**CONTENT AREAS**
Approaches to Learning

**MATERIALS**
- 5 large index cards
- Markers

# I. Helping During Child Care

## Why This Is Important:

- Young children are often interested in copying the actions of adults and may sometimes ask to help with household tasks.
- When thinking about giving children household chores to complete, adults should consider their interests. Allow them to talk about their plans for helping, and then give them opportunities to follow through.

### Beginning:

- With the children, make a heading on each of the index cards of an area in the house where they could accomplish a household task. You could have headings such as *Laundry, Kitchen, Outside,* and *Toy Area.*
- Under each heading, write down the children's ideas for the tasks they could complete. Under the kitchen heading, for example, you might write down "Setting the table" or "Wiping a counter."

### Middle:

- Let the children choose a task or two from the lists on the cards, and complete the tasks together.
- Talk with the children about what they are doing — remember that children need lots of practice to acquire skills!

### End:

- Find a place to post the lists of potential "child tasks."

### Follow-up Activities:

- Send home a family note describing household tasks children are interested in completing.
- Encourage the family to set up a routine in which everyone contributes by doing household chores together (for example, on Saturdays, Nathan takes the sheets off of his bed for laundering).

*Approaches to Learning*

# 2. Choosing Balls

## Why This Is Important:

- Children are not accustomed to having decision-making roles. On many occasions, especially in the areas of health and safety, it is necessary for adults to make decisions for children. This activity gives children an opportunity to have a decision-making role — to make choices about balls and hoops.

- Adults can show interest in the choices children make by commenting on their ideas, imitating their actions, and letting them be decision makers.

**CONTENT AREAS**
Approaches to Learning
Physical Development and Health

**MATERIALS**
- Variety of balls
- Hula-Hoops

## *Beginning:*

- Lay out the balls outside, and let the children experiment with the balls. Set the hoops behind you.

- Comment on what the children do with the balls, and imitate their actions. For example, you might say, "I see that the ball you are using bounces. I am going to see if this other ball bounces too."

## *Middle:*

- Introduce the hoops by putting them in front of you on the ground. Ask "How might you use these hoops with the balls?"

- Follow the children's lead, and imitate what they are doing with the balls and hoops. Play as a partner by joining a child's game, if invited.

- Describe what the children are doing with the balls and hoops, and then describe what you are doing with them. You might say, "I see you bouncing the ball inside the hoop. I'm trying to bounce the ball inside and then outside the hoop."

## *End:*

- Ask each child what he or she enjoyed doing most with the balls and hoops.

- Have the children help you put away the balls and hoops.

## Follow-up Activities:

- Ask the children to share their ideas about what could be used in place of the balls and hoops. For example, balls can be made from crumpled paper and tape; any container, such as a basket, could take the place of a hoop; and rope could be used to make an enclosure in which to throw a ball.

*Look around your family child care home and garage for items that can be used as balls and hoops — an old tire can make a perfect hoop!*

## 3. Planting Flowers

### Why This Is Important:

- Young children are developing a sense of community. As part of the community at home, at school, and in the neighborhood in which we each live, children are asked to take on responsibilities for the well-being of the community.

- This activity allows children to choose flower seeds to plant and water and transplant in a yard or flower box, when the plants are strong enough. Taking care of plants sends children a message about the importance in shared community responsibilities.

### *Beginning:*

- Talk with the children about flowering plants. You might ask, "Are there any in the yard?" or "Have you watched anyone plant flower seeds?"
- Let the children choose which seeds they would like to plant in the cups.

### *Middle:*

- Let the children put soil in the cups and plant the seeds. Use a paper cup for watering.
- Give each child a watering and growth chart. Encourage the children to draw what the cups and their contents look like today.

### *End:*

- Help the children find a place to put the cups where they will get sunlight.
- Find a place to display the watering and growth charts.

**CONTENT AREAS**
Approaches to Learning
Social Studies

**MATERIALS**
- 4 paper cups for each child
- 3 kinds of seeds
- Potting soil
- Ruler
- Weekly plant watering and growth chart, one for each child (see p. 13)

## Follow-up Activities:

- Discuss with the children the plants' growth. Help the children measure the plants' growth with a ruler and write the measurement in the box on the graph.
- Show family members the permanent spot outside where the plants are flourishing.
- Visit a larger community garden.

*Taking care of their seeds and watching them grow into flowers gives these children a sense of ownership and real pride.*

## Weekly Plant Watering and Growth Chart

Name _____

| My Plant Drawing | Date/Height | | Water | |
|---|---|---|---|---|
| | | | Yes | No |
| | | | | |
| | | | | |
| | | | | |
| | | | | |
| | | | | |
| | | | | |

# 4. Daily Routine Booklet

**CONTENT AREAS**
Approaches to Learning

Language, Literacy, and Communication

**MATERIALS**

- Booklet of the daily routine that includes the daily routine symbols used in the family child care home for the parts of the day such as arrivals, play or choice time, activity time, naptime, outside time, meals, and snacks: use a colored paper for the cover; prepare the daily routine symbols, one to each sheet of paper in chronological order; staple the booklet together

- Blank booklet for each child and family to create a "family routine" booklet (for activity to send home)

## Why This Is Important:

- Daily routines help meet young children's need for consistency and predictability. They also help children anticipate what is next and transition from one activity to the next.

- This booklet of the daily routine matches the symbols of the events that occur in the family child care home every day.

### Beginning:

- Share with the children the daily routine booklet, and ask them if they know what the booklet might be about.

### Middle:

- Let the children make comments about the daily routine booklet and follow their leads.

- Ask the children one or two questions about the daily routine to encourage a discussion about what happens during the day. For example, you might ask one of these questions:

  1. What do you like to do during play (or choice) time?
  2. What song do you like to sing during activity time?
  3. When it is cleanup time, how do you help clean up the toys?
  4. Which parts of our day do you like the most? What is something you do not like to do when you are here?

**Daily routine symbols** are picture representations that correspond to the different parts of your family child care routine. You may decide, for example, to depict activity time as a circle of smiley faces, representing the children sitting in a circle. Whatever you decide to use for your daily routine symbols, make sure that each symbol is meaningful to the children and remains the same for that particular part of the routine. Children's understanding of these symbols helps prepare them for reading in elementary school.

## End:

- After you have completed your conversation using the daily routine booklet, ask the children where it should be kept so that everyone can look at it.

## Activity to Send Home:

- Provide a blank booklet for each child and his or her family to create a family routine booklet. Ask the family to share the booklet with all of the children in your care during arrival time. Provide a designated space for the family routine booklets so that children can access them during the day.

*While sharing the daily routine booklet, talk to the children about the day's routine. Ask questions, such as "What parts of the day do you like most?"*

# Social and Emotional Development

**CONTENT AREAS**
Social and Emotional Development

Social Studies

**MATERIALS**
- Hand mirrors, one for each child and adult

# 5. Mirror, Mirror

## Why This Is Important:

- When children are able to express their feelings in words, it helps them gain some control over those feelings and the actions that accompany them.
- Adults can help children recognize emotions by acknowledging (naming) and accepting their feelings.

## *Beginning:*

- Give each child a hand mirror, and ask him or her to make some funny faces.
- Hold your own hand mirror, and copy the children's funny faces.
- Take turns making funny faces in the mirrors.

## *Middle:*

- Say something like "I wonder what it would look like if you had a sad face" to the children.
- Make faces representing other emotions.
- Describe a situation, and create a face to represent the corresponding emotion. For example, you might say, "I wonder what your face would look like if you got a new puppy."

## *End:*

- Make a sad face in the mirror, and say "Look how I feel now." Tell the children that you feel sad because it is time to put the mirrors away.
- Ask the children to help you think of happy things (to cheer you up) as you put the mirrors away.

## *Follow-up Activities:*

- Label your emotions and the children's emotions throughout the day. For example, you might say, "I'm feeling happy that the dishes are washed and I can read with you" or "You seem excited that Grandma is picking you up today."

*Social and Emotional Development*

- As you read stories to the children, talk about or ask about the characters' feelings. For example, if you are reading a story about Goldilocks and the three bears, you might say, "It looks like Baby Bear is crying. I think he's upset that Goldilocks ate his porridge. How do you think Papa Bear feels?"

*Adults can help children recognize emotions ("I miss my mommy!") by accepting and supporting their feelings.*

# 6. Child Care Photos

**CONTENT AREAS**
Social and Emotional Development

Social Studies

**MATERIALS**
- Photos of children and adults in your family child care program in a photo album
- Blank photo album (for follow-up activity)

## Why This Is Important:

- Positive relationships contribute to children's sense of competence and well-being.
- When children feel a part of a group (community), they learn to be open to the personal experiences of others within that group.

### Beginning:

- Show the children photos of themselves engaged in activities at your family child care home.
- Talk with the children about the photos by describing what you see in the photos. Ask the children open-ended questions about the pictures (for example, "What did you and Jayden do with the blocks after the picture was taken?"), and acknowledge what they say. For example, a child might say, "The road went all the way to the house area." You might respond, "The road stretched all the way to the house area, and then it stopped?"

### Middle:

- Encourage the children to have a conversation about who are in the pictures, what they are doing, and where they are playing.
- Talk about whether the children enjoy similar activities or have participated in similar experiences.

### End:

- Tell the children that you would like to make a photo album with pictures of the children at home. Talk to them about what kinds of photos they would like to bring in.

## Social and Emotional Development

### Follow-up Activities:

- Provide children with the opportunity to look at the photo album and talk about the people and events taking place.
- Continue to take pictures of the children during different parts of the day.
- Ask the families of children in your care to provide photos of their families for the children to look at and put in an album.

*This family child care provider took pictures of two boys experimenting with dump trucks to see which truck went faster down the slide. Later, the boys looked at the pictures together to recall what they discovered.*

# 7. Follow the Leader

**CONTENT AREAS**
Social and Emotional Development

**MATERIALS**
- Streamers, ribbon sticks, or scarves
- Instrumental music
- Music player

## Why This Is Important:

- Being a leader helps a child see him- or herself as a capable person whose ideas are valued by others.
- Children who feel competent have the self-confidence to take on new challenges.

### Beginning:

- Tell the children that you have some materials to use while moving to music.
- Turn on the music, and together explore ways of moving to the music with the materials.

### Middle:

- Copy the way one child is moving, and say "You are the leader. I am following you." Then choose another child's movements to copy, and encourage the other children to copy the "leader."
- Continue copying the children's movements, until each child has had a chance to be the leader.
- If the setting permits, take turns leading a parade around the house or yard.

### End:

- Have the children lead the parade back to put the materials away.

### Follow-up Activities:

- Play follow the leader during common transitions at your family child care (for example, as the children wash their hands for lunch or get ready to go outside).

*Social and Emotional Development*

# 8. Homemade Toothpaste

## Why This Is Important:

- Children are able to take care of some of their own needs. Children should be able to brush their teeth twice each day, with an adult's assistance. It is important for adults to model brushing teeth for their children.
- Children ages 6–7 are usually able to floss their teeth.
- Children's toothbrushes should be replaced every 3–4 months.

## *Beginning:*

- Tell the children that they are going to make some homemade toothpaste. Ask them if they brush their teeth with the help of a parent.
- Talk to the children about toothbrushing. Explain that brushing teeth removes plaque. You might say, "Plaque is sticky and comes from the food we eat mixed with germs. We brush our teeth to get rid of plaque, which makes holes in our teeth."

## *Middle:*

- Have the children mix the ingredients according to the rebus recipe.
- Hold the mirror as the children try out the toothpaste they made.
- Ask the children how the toothpaste tastes.

## *Ending:*

- Find a place to keep the homemade paste.
- The children might decide that the paste is too salty. In that case, talk about the kind of toothpaste they like.

## *Follow-up Activities:*

- Think about other needs that children can handle on their own (for example, washing the table after lunch).
- Children can also help follow other rebus recipe cards, such as one for making play dough.
- Send the toothpaste home with each child.

**CONTENT AREAS**

Social and Emotional Development

Science and Technology

Language, Literacy, and Communication

**MATERIALS**

- Small child's new toothbrush (one for each child)
- Mirror
- Rebus recipe card for the children to read (see p. 24)
- Ingredients for homemade toothpaste (see recipe below)
- Teaspoon
- Small airtight container for each child to keep the paste in (labeled with child's name)

**Toothpaste Recipe**

4 tsp. baking soda

1 tsp. salt

1 tsp. peppermint extract

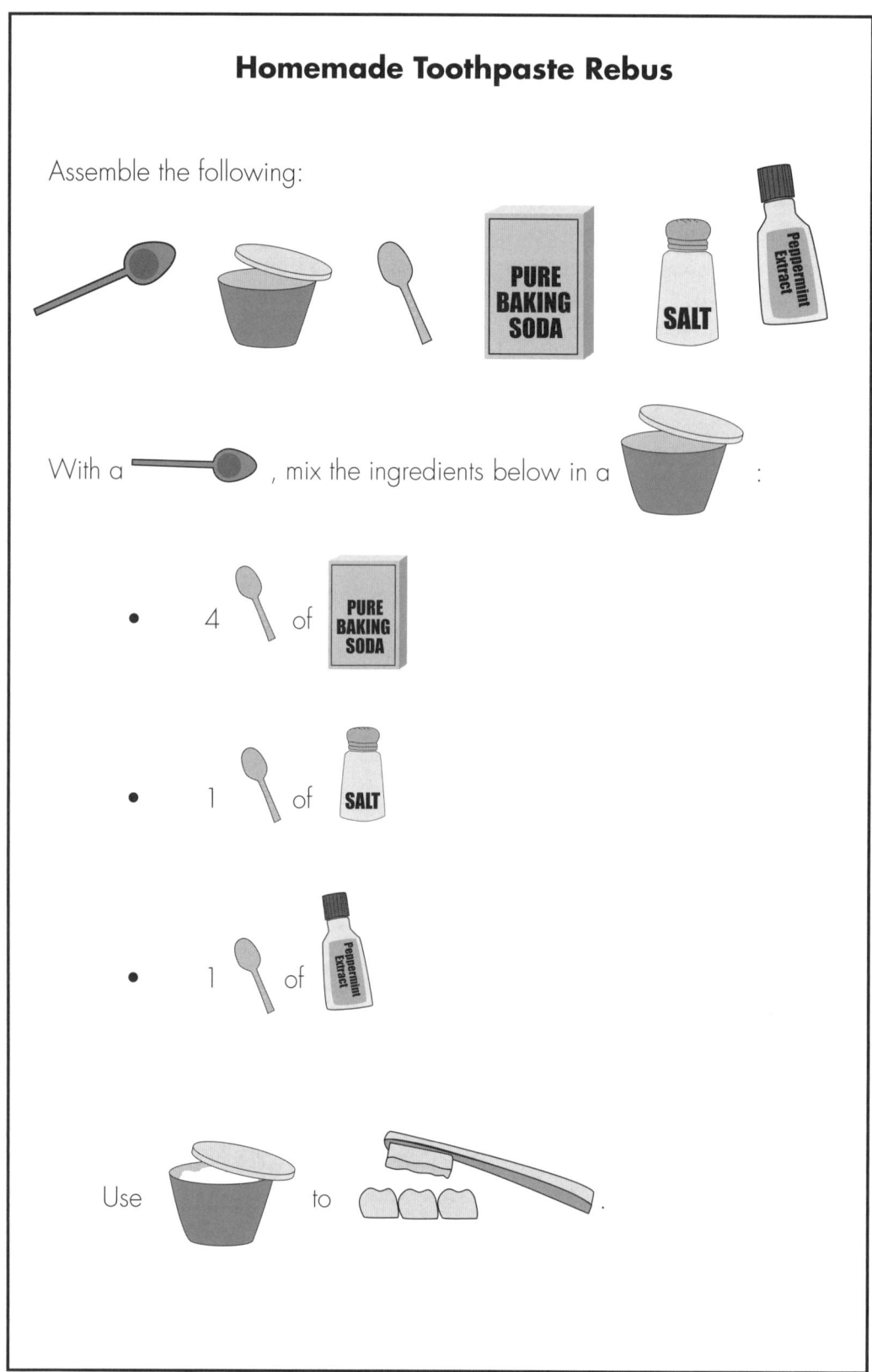

# Physical Development and Health

# 9. Ribbon Dancing

## Why This Is Important:

- When children hear music, they seem naturally to want to move to it. Adults can give children a wide variety of music to listen and move to.

- Moving to music gives children another way to express themselves and practice different ways of moving their bodies, which promotes physical development and body awareness.

### Beginning:

- Give each child a ribbon, and ask him or her to think of different ways to move it.

- Describe what the children do with the ribbon (say, for example, "You are making it go up and down"), and copy the children's movements.

### Middle:

- Play different selections of music, and move with the ribbons.

- When you change songs, ask questions such as "How does this music sound?" and "How will you move your ribbon to this music?"

- Continue to imitate the children as you move to the different songs.

### End:

- Let the children know when the last song is going to be played. Say that when the song ends, it will be time to put the ribbons away.

### Follow-up Activities:

- Find other objects that children can use to move with to music (for example, scarves, mittens, or metal soup cans [if the edges are smooth]).

**CONTENT AREAS**
Physical Development and Health
Creative Arts

**MATERIALS**
- Ribbons, each about 1 foot long
- 3–4 selections of music, preferably in different musical styles
- Music player

## 10. Batting Balloons

### Why This Is Important:

- As children move in their environment, they develop coordination, improve their physical conditioning, and gain self-confidence about their increasing physical abilities.

### *Beginning:*

- Show the child the balloons and bats at outside time, and say "I have brought these things today. What do you think we can do with them?"

### *Middle:*

- Watch and copy the way the children use the materials.
- Use the bat to hit the balloon in the air.
- Help the children hit the balloon back and forth between players.

### *End:*

- Tell the children that it is time to go back inside.
- Encourage the children to help you put the materials away by batting the balloon toward the door.

### *Follow-up Activities:*

- Think of other lightweight items for children to toss, kick, or bat, such as beach balls, scarves, rolled socks, and other items to use as bats (see the Materials list).

**CONTENT AREAS**
Physical Development and Health

**MATERIALS**

- 9-inch balloons (*Note:* If popped balloons might be a choking hazard in the family child care home, use large beach balls or put balloons inside a nylon stocking to keep small pieces from smaller children.)
- Foam bats (you can also use rolled newspaper, paper plates attached to sticks, or paper towel tubes as bats)

*Hitting a ball with a bat helps children develop their hand-eye coordination.*

*Preschool Activities for Family Child Care*

**CONTENT AREAS**
Physical Development and Health

**MATERIALS**
- 2 chairs
- Mop handle or broom

# II. Animal Moves

## Why This Is Important:

- Children are physically active. They are able to create movements to imitate their favorite animals (Laney, for example, likes to stretch just like Angel, her cat).

- As children move like their favorite animals, adults can comment on and label their actions. An adult might say, "Laney, it looks like you are stretching just like Angel does after a nap in the doorway."

- Children often enjoy movement challenges.

## *Beginning:*

- Tell the children that you are thinking of an animal, and ask each child to think of an animal too.

- Move like the animal you are thinking of and walk around the room. Ask the children to move around the room like the animal they are thinking of.

- Tell the children that you are thinking of another animal and then move like that second animal. Ask the children to also think of and move like another animal. Repeat this with a third animal/animal movement.

- Have a child assist you in setting up the broom or mop handle between the seats of two chairs.

## *Middle:*

- Say "Let's see if we can move like our favorite animal and go under the broom handle."

- Move like your favorite animal, and try to go *under* the broom handle. Ask the children to move like their favorite animal and try to go *under* the broom handle.

- After three rounds, see if you can move like your favorite animal and go *over* the broom handle. (If the children are not tall enough to go over the broom handle between the two chairs, place it on the floor between the two chairs.)

Physical Development and Health

- Ask the children what other animal movements they could create to go under or over the broom handle. Try out some of these actions.

*End:*

- Have the children assist in putting away the broom handle and chairs.
- Make a note about the children's suggestions for movements under and over the broom handle.

*Follow-up Activities:*

- Play this game outdoors with the children, and continue to describe the children's actions as they go over or under the broom handle.

*Children love to test their physical abilities, including how fast they can run down a hill!*

*Preschool Activities for Family Child Care*

# 12. Following the String

## Why This Is Important:

- Children enjoy moving their bodies; they roll, crawl, run, gallop, jump, hop, and skip.
- Physical movement builds coordination. As children become adept at balance and coordination, their self-confidence grows.

## *Beginning:*

- Take the children and your ball of string out in the yard.
- Tie the string to the bottom of a tree trunk. Run the string along the ground to other obstacles in the yard (for example, unwind more of the string across the lawn and under the picnic table and along the ground and over the sidewalk).

## *Middle:*

- Follow the children as they move through the obstacle course that you have made.
- Travel through the obstacle course several times in different ways with the children (for example, run, crawl, and hop along the string).

## *End:*

- Let the children help you collect the string and roll it back up in the ball.

## *Follow-up Activities:*

- Think of some other ways to make an obstacle course in your yard or nearby in a park, or even in an open space in your home (for example, you can use a Hula-Hoop to jump in or out of or milk crates to run between).

**CONTENT AREAS**
Physical Development and Health

**MATERIALS**
- Ball of string or skein of yarn

*You can also do this activity in an open space in your home with string or rope.*

# Language, Literacy, and Communication

# 13. Rhyming Objects

## Why This Is Important:

- Rhymes help children hear the sounds that make up words. Specifically, they help children identify and isolate word endings that sound the same.

**CONTENT AREAS**
Language, Literacy, and Communication

**MATERIALS**
- Cloth drawstring bag, paper bag, or basket
- Familiar objects with names that rhyme with other objects found in the house (for example, rocks, socks, and blocks; moons, balloons, and spoons; dogs, frogs, and [Lincoln] logs)

### Beginning:

- Put enough objects in the bag so that each child will get a turn to pull one out.
- Ask the children to guess what is in the bag. Let each child pull an object out of the bag and name it.

### Middle:

- Ask the children to find other objects in the house that rhyme with the item they pulled from the bag. If the child is unable to name a rhyming object, model by naming a rhyming object. For example, you might say, "Let's find objects that rhyme with *rock*. Look…here's a sock and a clock. They both rhyme with *rock*."
- If the children are enjoying this activity, put all of the items back in the bag and let them continue to pull objects from the bag, name them, and find something that rhymes with those items.

### End:

- Have the children help you put all of the objects back in the bag or in their appropriate place in the home.

### Follow-up Activities:

- Do a scavenger hunt with objects whose names rhyme in your home. For example, you might ask the children, "Can you find something that rhymes with this lamp?"

## 14. Alliteration I Spy

### Why This Is Important:

- This activity builds children's awareness of initial sounds in words when two or more words in a row begin with the same sound (for example, "tick, tack, toe" or "goodness gracious!"). This repetition of initial sounds is called *alliteration*.

**CONTENT AREAS**
Language, Literacy, and Communication

**MATERIALS**
- Storybook that includes alliteration, for example:
  - *The Baby Beebee Bird* by Diane Redfield Massie
  - *The Duchess Bakes a Cake* by Virginia Kahl
  - *Sheep on a Ship* by Nancy Shaw
  - *Silly Sally* by Audrey Wood
- Roll of masking tape
- Marker

### *Beginning:*

- Read the story with the children, pointing out the common beginning sounds.

### *Middle:*

- Say something like "Let's play a little game with the beginning sounds of words. I spy something in this room that begins with a /d/ sound." If, for example, a child identifies "door," put a piece of tape with the letter *d* on the door. Then you might ask, "Can you think of other things in the house that begin with a /d/?" Label the objects with the letter *d*. If a child gives an incorrect answer, say something like "You named the /s/ sound in *sofa*. What other things can you see that start with the /s/ sound?"

- Continue the game with other beginning sounds.

### *End:*

- With the children, remove the tape from the objects that you have labeled.

### *Follow-up Activities:*

- Play I spy with beginning sounds at mealtimes. For example, if you are serving peas at lunchtime, you might say, "I spy something that begins with a /p/ sound, like *plate*."

**CONTENT AREAS**
Language, Literacy, and Communication

**MATERIALS**
- Collection of materials that make noise (for example, keys on a ring, cellophane, newspaper, wooden blocks, small tins, chopsticks, an alarm clock, bells) in a basket
- Small tape recorder

# 15. Sounds, Sounds, Sounds

## Why This Is Important:

- Activities like these will encourage children to hear, locate, and name environmental sounds. These activities set the stage for hearing and identifying the subtle sounds that make up words.

### Beginning:

- Ask the children to find out what kinds of noises the objects make.

### Middle:

- Let the children experiment with the materials. Talk with them about the sounds they hear. Make some sounds with the objects and comment on the sounds you hear.
- Using a tape recorder, record the sounds that the children make with the objects.
- After the children have experimented with the materials, have each child choose his or her favorite sound.

### End:

- Have the children return the materials to the collection basket by identifying the sounds of the objects from the tape recorder.

### Follow-up Activities:

- Take a walk through the neighborhood and talk about the sounds children hear. Help them write down all of the outdoor sounds they heard so they can share the list with their family.

*Language, Literacy, and Communication*

# 16. Making Connections

## Why This Is Important:

**CONTENT AREAS**
Language, Literacy, and Communication

**MATERIALS**
- Each child's favorite object in the family child care home

- To understand a story that is being told or read to them, children need to make connections between what they hear and things they already know. To understand what a story is about, they need to connect the objects, characters, and events in a story to things in their own lives. As a story unfolds, they also need to link the events of the story together. To do this, they have to figure out what goes on in every story event, keep each event in mind, and then connect the series of events into a coherent story.

- This activity helps children make the connections necessary to understand a story narrative.

## Beginning:

- Ask each child to describe the favorite object and how he or she plays with it.

## Middle:

- Make up a story with the child about the object that includes three ideas. Think about incorporating the child's known interests, family members, and neighborhood or friends from your family child care. For example, if the child brings you his favorite car, you might make up this story with three ideas:

    *Idea #1:* "Jonas got into his red car and decided to drive it to the park."

    *Idea #2:* "On the way to the park, he saw his mom pushing his sister Kaya in the stroller. They were walking to the park too."

    *Idea #3:* "When Jonas arrived at the park, he drove until he found his favorite slide. He parked the car near the slide. He jumped out of the car and went right up the steps on the slide and whoosh…down the slide he slid."

## End:

- Let each child who wants to retell his or her story and then put the object away to transition to the next activity.

## Follow-up Activities:

- Look at photograph albums with pictures you have taken of the children in your care. Let the children talk about the photos and what they remember about events. Or, let each child choose a photo in the album to make up a story about.

*To understand a story, children need to connect what they are hearing about and looking at to things they know about in their own lives.*

*Language, Literacy, and Communication*

# 17. Animal Cubes

## Why This Is Important:

- Giving children many opportunities to speak and listen helps get them ready to read and write when they go to school.
- This activity with animal cubes allows children to make choices and to talk about what they know.

## *Beginning:*

- Encourage the children to choose pictures to glue onto each side of their cube.
- Help the children cut out and glue the pictures to fit their cube (they may be able to do this by themselves).

## *Middle:*

- Tell the children that you are going to take turns rolling the cubes and talking about the animals in the pictures.
- Ask for a volunteer to go first. After the child rolls his or her cube, ask the child to talk about the animal in the picture.
- Let each child have a chance to roll his or her cube and talk about an animal. Take a turn yourself, and talk about one of the animals.

## *End:*

- When each child has had a chance to talk about one or two animals, help the children find a place to store the cubes so they can be used at another time.

## *Activity to Send Home:*

- Send home an empty cube for the family to create using pictures that the child enjoys.

**CONTENT AREAS**
Language, Literacy, and Communication

**MATERIALS**

- Large cube for each child, which can be made from a half-gallon juice carton or from a wooden block (have an extra one for an activity to send home)
- Glue
- Scissors
- Old magazines or post cards with pictures of animals

# 18. Story Bag

**CONTENT AREAS**
Language, Literacy, and Communication

**MATERIALS**
- Objects from a familiar storybook, such as the items found in *Good Night, Gorilla* by Peggy Rathmann (*Note:* Be sure that you have enough objects so that each child gets to choose one object.)
- Familiar storybook the objects are from
- Pillowcase or bag to hold objects

## Why This Is Important:

- Retelling a familiar story engages children in the complex thinking needed to understand a story and re-create it in their minds.
- Retelling also allows children to enter the lives of story characters and to connect their own experiences to the characters' experiences.
- This activity will help children retell a story, putting their thoughts into words and letting them try out new words and ideas.

## *Beginning:*

- Read the story to the children, keeping the items in the bag.

## *Middle:*

- After you have finished sharing the story, give each child a chance to pull out one item from the bag and talk about where he or she saw it in the storybook and the story events that are connected to that item.
- Ask the children which item appeared first, second, third, and so forth.

## *End:*

- Have the children help you put the items back inside the bag.

## *Follow-up Activities:*

- Repeat the activity with another familiar story that the children like.

*Language, Literacy, and Communication*

# 19. Hopscotch With Letter Links

## Why This Is Important:

- Through their experiences with books and print, children recognize that written words are connected to spoken words and carry meaning.

- Children are also beginning to expand upon their letter (alphabetic) knowledge. They are beginning to understand that letters make up words as they read their own scribbles.

### *Beginning:*

- Let the children choose enough names/pictures that they know or recognize to make a hopscotch board.

### *Middle:*

- Set up the hopscotch board with the children, taping down the names/pictures.

- Play hopscotch with the children, calling out the names (or letters, if the children can recognize them) while playing. (*Note:* If a child cannot hop on one foot, encourage him or her to use both feet.)

### *End:*

- Together, gather the papers used for the hopscotch board(s) to put in a basket.

### *Follow-up Activities:*

- Leave copies of all of the names/letter-linked pictures in a basket so that the children can play this game at other times.

**CONTENT AREAS**
Language, Literacy, and Communication

**MATERIALS**
- Letter-linked pictures with names* of children printed on 8" x 11" sheets of paper (you may want to laminate these)
- Markers (for playing hopscotch)
- Tape
- Basket

*In this example, the child's name is paired with a picture of an automobile, which starts with the same letter and sound as Audrey.*

---

*Letter links is a name-learning system that pairs a child's printed name with a picture of a word that starts with the same letter and sound, for example, the name Delia and a picture of a deer. For more information, see *Letter Links: Alphabet Learning With Children's Names* (2003) from HighScope Press or Letter Links Online at www.highscope.org.

# 20. Wordless Picture Books

**CONTENT AREAS**
Language, Literacy, and Communication

**MATERIALS**
- Wordless picture book, for example:
  - *Bears* by Ruth Krauss and Maurice Sendak
  - *A Boy, a Dog, and a Frog* by Mercer Mayer
  - *Changes, Changes* by Pat Hutchins
  - *Flotsam* by David Wiesner
  - *Good Night, Gorilla* by Peggy Rathmann
  - *Tuba Lessons* by T.C. Bartlett
  - *Mama* by Jeanette Winter
  - *Pancakes for Breakfast* by Tomie dePaola
  - *Rainstorm* by Barbara Lehman

## Why This Is Important:

- Children begin their reading journey by reading pictures.
- This activity gives children an opportunity to tell a story by reading the pictures.
- When reading a picture book to children, adults can invite conversation by asking a question or making a comment, such as "I wonder what you see on this page." Adults can encourage children to talk about objects, animals, and people they see in illustrations on the cover and in the pages of the book.

## *Beginning:*

- Let the children hold and touch the book. Begin by asking the children what they think will happen in this book based on what they see on the cover.

## *Middle:*

- Let the children describe for you what they see on the pages. Ask them what they think will happen next. Converse with the children about things in the pictures they have seen or played with themselves.

## *End:*

- Ask the children what they think the character might do after the story ends.

## *Follow-up Activities:*

- Have children make their own picture books to read to you.

---

### How to Make a Picture Book

- Fold three sheets of 8½" x 11" paper in half. Use a piece of colored construction paper for the cover.
- Staple the pages together, at the crease.

# Mathematics

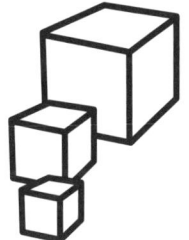

# 21. Graphing Favorite Fruits

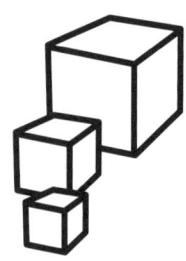

**CONTENT AREAS**
Mathematics
Social Studies

**MATERIALS**
- Paper
- Markers
- Pictures of fruits (*Note:* Be sure to include duplicate pictures of the same fruit [for example, 3 pictures of an apple].)

## Why This Is Important:

- Young children are developing what mathematicians call *number sense*. They are beginning to understand that numerals represent numbers of objects and are recognizing what has more or fewer, is bigger or smaller, and so on. Young children are also beginning to estimate and calculate differences in quantity.

- Children also know that others have different tastes and interests.

## *Beginning:*

- Lay out the pictures of fruit.
- Talk about which is your favorite fruit.
- Ask the children which are their favorites. For instance, you might ask, "Why is it your favorite?" Draw out the children's reasons with open-ended questions and comments (for example, a child might like the fruit's color, texture, or taste, or just because it goes well with ice cream).

## *Middle:*

- Make a graph using your favorite fruit and the children's favorite fruits (see sample graph on the facing page).
- Ask the children "Which fruit seems to be the favorite? Which fruits are left out?"

## *End:*

- Put the graph in a visible place in your home so family members can weigh in as they come for pickup time.

## *Follow-up Activities:*

- Ask the children what other things they can think of to make a graph for (examples might include favorite cookies, favorite sports, food they don't like), and repeat this activity.

## Our Favorite Fruits

| 👧👦 | 🍇 | 🍎 | 🍓 | 🍊 |
|---|---|---|---|---|
| Lucia |  |  |  | X |
| Sasha | X |  |  |  |
| José | X |  |  |  |
| Ethan |  |  | X |  |
|  |  |  |  |  |
|  |  |  |  |  |
|  |  |  |  |  |

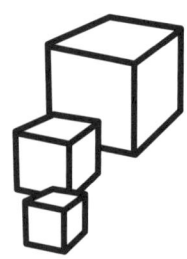

**CONTENT AREAS**
Mathematics

**MATERIALS**
- 10 small people or animal figures
- Scarf or other long piece of fabric

# 22. Ten in the Bed

## Why This Is Important:

- Rote counting is saying numbers in order by memory. This is one aspect of learning to count.
- Children also need to manipulate small numbers of real objects (touch, handle, move, sort, and group them) to develop an understanding of what the numbers mean.
- Children develop an understanding of how numbers work by solving different types of number problems as they work directly with real objects.

## Beginning:

- Lay the scarf out on a table, and place the figures on top.
- Explain to the children that the scarf is a bed and the figures are sleeping.
- Ask "How many are sleeping in the bed?"

## Middle:

- Sing "Ten Little Monkeys" with the children, beginning with "There were 10 (or other number) in the bed and the little one said…"
- Ask a child to make one of the figures roll off the bed.
- Repeat the song or chant a few times. Ask another child to say whether one, two, or three figures should roll off and have a different child make one of the figures fall off.
- Ask the children to predict how many figures will be left on the bed.

## End:

- When all the figures are off the bed, ask the children to help you count them (out loud) as you put them away.

## Follow-up Activities:

- Ask the children to think of objects that could be used to reenact the story again (such as a dish towel and spoons).

# 23. Looking for Numbers

## Why This Is Important:

- Just as we want children to learn the ABCs, we also want them to learn numerals.
- Adults can help children learn numerals by calling attention to them in the environment and showing children how they are useful in their lives.

## *Beginning:*

- Display the items and, with the children's help, identify the numbers.
- Ask the children to think of other things that have numbers on them.

## *Middle:*

- Look around the room or house for objects with numbers.
- Encourage the children to point to and name the numbers.
- Point out and name unknown numbers.

## *End:*

- Tell the children that they are going to look for one last number — outside the house or apartment.
- With the children, look for the house address or apartment number near the door.

## *Follow-up Activities:*

- When you go on a neighborhood walk or take a field trip, call attention to numbers throughout the environment. Some examples include numbered houses or apartments, gas station signs, highway exit signs, and elevator buttons.

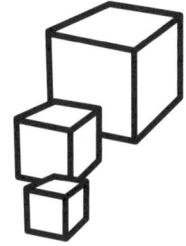

**CONTENT AREAS**
Mathematics

**MATERIALS**

- Selection of objects that have numbers on them (for example, phone, calculator, numbered race car)

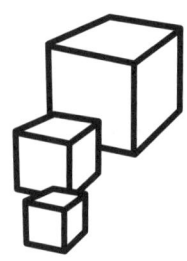

**CONTENT AREAS**
Mathematics

**MATERIALS**

- Homemade puzzle for each child
  - Picture of familiar object, such as an animal from an old calendar or magazine
  - Cardboard or cardstock
  - Clear contact paper for laminating
- Envelope or folder for each child to hold puzzle pieces; envelope should be labeled with child's name

**How to Make a Puzzle**

- Attach the picture to cardboard or cardstock.
- Cut out the picture into 4–10 pieces (depending on the developmental level of the child).
- Cover each piece with clear contact paper (or laminate) to make sturdier puzzle pieces.

# 24. Picture Puzzles

## Why This Is Important:

- Putting puzzles together helps children develop spatial reasoning, which is a component of geometry and an important aspect of mechanical skills.
- Children have to have an idea of what an object looks like (picture it in their minds) to piece it back together.

### Beginning:

- Tell the children that you have some homemade puzzles to use today.
- Hand the child a piece of one of the puzzles from his or her envelope, and ask the child to guess what the picture might be. Ask "How do you know that?"

### Middle:

- Give each child the appropriate envelope, and encourage the child to piece the puzzle together.
- Use direction words, such as *turn* and *flip*, and position words, such as *above*, *next to*, and *underneath*.

### End:

- When the puzzles are complete, talk about whether the children's initial guesses about their picture were correct.
- Have the children put the puzzle pieces back in their envelope and put them in a place where they can use them at another time.

### Follow-up Activities:

- Suggest that parents make (or help their children make) puzzles out of the fronts of cereal or cracker boxes.

## 25. Play Dough and Marbles

### Why This Is Important:

- Rote counting is saying numbers in order by memory, one aspect of learning to count.
- Children learn to understand what numbers mean by touching and moving real objects.
- Children often judge quantity based on appearance.

### *Beginning:*

- Pass out one play dough portion to each child (save one portion for you). Say something like "I have special play dough today. See if you can find out what makes it special."
- Acknowledge the children's discovery of the hidden objects.

### *Middle:*

- Make a general comment about the quantity of objects discovered. For example, you might say, "You are finding many marbles" or "That looks like a lot of marbles."
- Remove the objects from your own play dough and line them up in front of you. Say something like "I have a lot too. I wonder how many?" (Children may start counting their marbles or your marbles either by rote or with one-to-one correspondence.)
- Model counting your marbles, comparing quantities, or making sets of different amounts based on the developmental level of each child.

### *End:*

- Have the children help you remove all the marbles from the play dough and put the materials away.

### *Follow-up Activities:*

- Find fun and unusual things to count, such as freckles on an arm, buttons on a shirt, or steps it takes to go from one place to another.

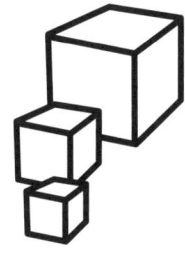

**CONTENT AREAS**
Mathematics

**MATERIALS**
- Play dough portions (one for each child and adult) with marbles, stones, or similarly small objects hidden inside

### Recipe for Play Dough

4 cups flour

1 cup salt

4 cups water

4 tbsp. vegetable oil

2 tbsp. cream of tartar

Food coloring or 1 package of Kool-Aid

- In a large saucepan, mix the first 5 ingredients.
- Cook mixture at medium-low on the stove until the dough comes away from the pan's edges. Remove from heat and cool.
- Knead, add food coloring or package of Kool-Aid, and store in an airtight container.

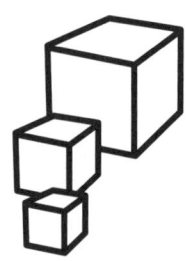

**CONTENT AREAS**
Mathematics

Physical Development and Health

**MATERIALS**
- Paper
- Pencils

# 26. Measuring by Leaps and Bounds

## Why This Is Important:

- This activity will give children practice estimating, measuring, and counting with nonstandard units of measure (for example, hands, feet, shoes).

## Beginning:

- Say something like "Let's guess how many hops to the garage (or wall or fence)."
- Then ask "What else could we measure with different kinds of steps (giant, baby, hops, leaps)?"

## Middle:

- On the paper, help each child record his or her estimate of how many _____ to the _____.
- Let each child measure with steps, hops, leaps, or lengths of his or her arm.
- Record the child's answer next to his or her guess.

## End:

- Look at the results of what the children estimated and what was actually measured.
- Ask "What did we learn?"

## Follow-up Activities:

- Let the children use a hand or foot to measure in addition to using a yardstick or ruler.

# 27. Shape Hunt

## Why This Is Important:

- Children are keen observers.
- Children organize information into categories based on specific characteristics (such as shape).
- Recognizing shapes is an element of geometry.

## *Beginning:*

- Show the children the large shape.
- Name the shape, and talk about its features. You might, for example, talk about how a circle is curved, has no points or corners, and is round like a ball.

## *Middle:*

- With the children, look around the room or house for other items of that shape.
- When developmentally appropriate, you might, with the children, compile a list of the items you see in the room or house that matches the shape.

## *End:*

- Ask the children where the shape could be stored for them to use again.

## *Follow-up Activities:*

- Repeat this activity with a different shape.
- Look for shapes in other environments, such as outdoors.

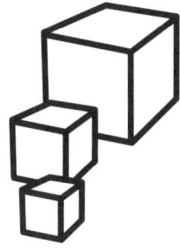

**CONTENT AREAS**
Mathematics
Science and Technology

**MATERIALS**
- Large circle, triangle, or rectangle cut out of cardstock or other sturdy material (choose one shape)
- Paper and pencil

# Creative Arts

# 28. Painting With Watercolors

## Why This Is Important:

- Children need time to explore materials (such as paint) before they can actually paint something recognizable.
- In the exploration stage, children are more interested in the process of using the paint and less concerned about how their final picture looks.
- As children become more familiar with art materials, they gradually move from accidental discovery (such as making a line and deciding it looks like a snake) to intentional representations.

## *Beginning:*

- Introduce the watercolor pallet, and explore with the children what happens when you add water to the paint.
- Imitate the children as they explore paint and water on paper.

## *Middle:*

- Listen to the children describe their work. Make comments about what you see the children doing, such as, "You're rubbing your paintbrush around and around in the paint."
- Use your paintbrush in different ways to create different types of lines. Describe your own actions and the lines you make. For example, you might brush up and down very fast and call your lines *zigzags*.

## *End:*

- Say one thing you like about painting as you put away your materials.
- Ask the children if they would like to display their pictures in the special place you have provided for their work.

**CONTENT AREAS**
Creative Arts

**MATERIALS**

- Watercolors
- Paintbrushes
- Cups with water
- Paper
- Newspaper to cover work surface
- Smock for each child

## Follow-up Activities:

- Use paintbrushes with plain water on the sidewalk.

*Before children make intentional representations, they need time to explore the materials used for painting.*

**CONTENT AREAS**
Creative Arts

**MATERIALS**
- Crayons
- Plain paper

# 29. Drawing With Crayons

## Why This Is Important:

- Early representations consist of simple forms that gradually become more detailed.
- Adults can encourage children to do their own artwork and describe what they have drawn.
- Adults should avoid making models for children to copy.

## Beginning:

- Set out the paper and crayons. Point out to the children that the paper is plain, so they can use their imagination to make different types of marks, shapes, or other representations.

## Middle:

- Observe the way children draw on paper.
- Imitate the types of lines or shapes the children make, and describe what you are doing. For example, you might say, "I'm making fast lines that go up and down, just like you are making."
- If a child is making a detailed representation, help him or her think about other details to add, such as straight or curly hair on a person, apples on a tree, or a door or windows on a house.
- Make and describe other types of lines or shapes, such as wavy, thick, or curved lines; circles; or triangles. Use words to compare lines and shapes, such as *large* and *small, dark* and *light,* and *squiggly* and *straight.*

## End:

- When the children are finished coloring, say "Tell me about your picture."
- Accept the children's descriptions or explanations. For example, a child may call a page full of colorful squiggles a dinosaur. You might say, "Yes, you used lots of squiggly lines to make a dinosaur."

## Creative Arts

- Ask the children if they would like to display their pictures in the house.

## *Follow-up Activities:*

- Make a book of the children's pictures.

*If the child has a hard time coming up with something to draw, suggest that he draw something that he did that day, like this child did — a picture of his mother and him going to the family child care home!*

# 30. Art Appreciation

**CONTENT AREAS**
Creative Arts

Language, Literacy, and Communication

**MATERIALS**
- Post cards of paintings, such as Mary Cassatt's *The Boating Party,* Claude Monet's *The Artist's Garden at Vetheuil,* and Pierre-Auguste Renoir's *A Girl With a Watering Can*
- 3 different kinds of paper (for example, newsprint, manila paper, or drawing paper)
- Chalk
- Pencils
- Old newspapers for protecting a surface during drawing (*Note:* This is activity can be done outdoors, just as many artists paint.)

## Why This Is Important:

- The arts play an important role in cognitive, motor, language, and social-emotional development. As children engage in the artistic process, they learn to observe, organize, and interpret experiences.
- Children's representations will develop from simple to complex; their representations grow from their real experiences. Every child's representations are unique.
- Children are able to appreciate as well as make art.

### Beginning:

- Lay out the post cards, and let the children look at, touch, and talk about the ones they like.
- Talk about what they see. Ask "What do you think is happening in the picture?" Talk about colors and textures.

### Middle:

- Let the children choose paper, chalk, and pencils.
- Be sure to use the materials yourself. Imitate what the children do with the materials.
- Talk about textures and colors in the children's work. Let the children take the lead.

### End:

- Finish the activity by finding a place to display the artwork.
- Let the children assist with putting away the materials so they can be used at another time.

*Creative Arts*

## Follow-up Activities:

- Think about the possibilities for things for the children to use as paper to draw on — newspapers, paper towels, and old magazines often work well. You can also use Q-Tips for painting too.

*Young children's representations develop from simple to complex.*

**CONTENT AREAS**
Creative Arts
Science and Technology

**MATERIALS**
- Heavyweight paper
- Glue
- Variety of collage materials with different textures (for example, cotton, sand paper, fabric pieces, feathers, aluminum foil)

# 31. Texture Collage

## Why This Is Important:

- Children use all their senses to sort objects by different properties.
- Classification means grouping or organizing things by a common trait. Children classify things to help them organize their understanding of the world.

### Beginning:

- Introduce the collage materials, and encourage the children to describe them. Model descriptive words such as *soft*, *shiny*, or *bumpy*.

### Middle:

- Use paper and glue to create a collage with the materials, and encourage the children to create a collage as well.
- As you are working, continue to describe materials. For example, you might say, "I'm choosing soft things."
- Encourage the children to think of other things in the house that are similar to the materials they are using. You might say, "This aluminum foil is shiny, and the kitchen faucet is shiny."

### End:

- Have the children help you put away unused materials.
- Talk with the children about their collages. Say something like "Let's look at your collage together. Tell me what you did."

### Follow-up Activities:

- Go on a treasure hunt around the house. Find items with similar attributes (for example, things that are soft, shiny, or made of wood).

# Science and Technology

# 32. It's in the Bag

**CONTENT AREAS**
Science and Technology

**MATERIALS**
- Cloth tote bag (or any opaque bag)
- Small toys from your family child care home, which are familiar to the children

## Why This Is Important:

- Children use all their senses to explore and learn about the physical world.
- Children must remember the features of familiar objects (by forming images in their brains) and compare those memories to the objects they are touching.

### Beginning:

- Place the toys out on a table and, with the children, identify each toy.
- Remove the toys from the table, and put them in the bag.

### Middle:

- Ask each child to put his or her hand into the bag and feel the toy inside.
- Ask each child to describe what he or she feels and to guess which toy it is.
- Ask "How did you know it was that toy?"

### End:

- Let each child take a turn describing features of a toy as you put them away. Model for the children how you would describe the features of a toy. You might say, for example, "I'm putting away the toy with four wheels."

### Follow-up Activities:

- Look for opportunities to describe objects for the children to guess. For example, when preparing lunch in the kitchen, you might say, "We need some fruit that is long and has a yellow peel."

## 33. Magnets

### Why This Is Important:

- Children are natural scientists, observing and investigating what things are made of and how things work.
- Part of "doing" science is predicting and then testing ideas to discover the properties of objects and how objects can interact with one another.

### *Beginning:*

- Introduce the magnet wand or magnet, and explain that it attracts some objects that are made of metal.
- Place the assortment of materials on the table, and say "Some of these things will stick to a magnet. How can we find out which ones are magnetic?"

### *Middle:*

- Give each child a magnet wand or magnet to use to determine which objects are magnetic (not all things made of metal are magnetic).
- Ask the children to predict whether an object is magnetic. Ask "How do you know?" to learn more about the children's thinking.

### *End:*

- Before putting the magnets away, ask the children to look around the room for two other objects they think are magnetic. (Be sure children do not put a magnet on a computer or television screen.)

### *Follow-up Activities:*

- With the children, talk about what objects are made of (for example, wood, plastic, metal, cloth).
- Play I spy, and give clues about the properties of an object (for example, "I spy something that is red and made of wood").

**CONTENT AREAS**
Science and Technology

**MATERIALS**
- Magnet wands or other large magnets, one for each child
- Assorted materials (magnetic and nonmagnetic)

**CONTENT AREAS**
Science and Technology

**MATERIALS**

- 6 plastic water bottles filled with different items (for example, salt, sand, dried beans or rice, buttons, nuts and bolts) to make different sounds when shaken

# 34. Listening to Shakers

## Why This Is Important:

- Children need opportunities to use all their senses to learn about the world.
- When adults ask children to pay attention to sounds in the environment, they sharpen their sense of sound.

## *Beginning:*

- Show the children the water bottles, and talk about how each sounds different when shaken.

## *Middle:*

- Ask one child to close his or her eyes while you shake one of the bottles.
- Ask the child to guess which bottle you shook. Ask "How did you know?"
- Switch roles — have each child shake a bottle while you close your eyes.

## *End:*

- Ask the children to help you put the bottles away.

## *Follow-up Activities:*

- Make a shaker with the children using pebbles, buttons, or coins.
- Take a "sound walk" with the children to listen to sounds in the neighborhood.

# 35. Soapy Suds

## Why This Is Important:

- Science is an active process where children observe the physical world, investigate how things work, test their own ideas, and come to their own conclusions.
- Children need to handle and explore materials to discover the properties of those materials and how certain actions can cause materials to change.

### Beginning:

- Pour water into the dish tub(s) so it is no more than 1 inch high.
- Tell the children that you would like to make lots of soap suds. Ask "How do you think we can do that?"

### Middle:

- Pour soap onto a sponge, and just place it in the water without swishing it.
- Ask "Now what do we have to do?"
- Encourage the children to explore using the sponges (for example, by squeezing them) to make lots of soap suds.
- Encourage the children to describe what they are doing to make the bubbles.

### End:

- Have the children help you rinse out the tub(s) and the sponges in the sink.

### Follow-up Activities:

- Put soap onto a washcloth to see if this produces as many bubbles as the soap on the sponge.

**CONTENT AREAS**
Science and Technology

**MATERIALS**
- Large dish tub or 2 or 3 smaller tubs
- 2–3 sponges for each child and adult who is participating
- Baby shampoo
- Water
- Smock for each child

**CONTENT AREAS**
Science and Technology

**MATERIALS**

- 6 sand timers, some of different sizes
- 2–3 tubs of small stones, rice, sand, or beads
- Paper or plastic cups (7 for each child and adult)
- Paper and pencil

---

**Homemade Sand Timer**

To make your own sand timer, attach two clear plastic bottles with a Tornado Tube and fill the bottle with sand or salt. (Tornado Tubes can be purchased through teacher supply catalogs.)

---

# 36. Using Timers

## Why This Is Important:

- Time is an abstract concept for young children; they measure time in concrete and sensory ways. As children form mental images, they are able to remember past events and anticipate future events.
- In this activity, the children will relate lengths of time to an event.

## *Beginning:*

- Bring out the sand timers for the children to explore.
- Ask the children to predict which timer empties faster.

## *Middle:*

- Show the children the tubs filled with stones (or other material). Ask each child to predict how many cups he or she can fill with stones before the sand has run out of the timer.
- Pass out the cups, turn the timers over, and see how close each child comes to his or her prediction.
- Have the children use the sand timer to time you as you attempt to fill the cups.
- Ask the children for ideas about what else to time. A child might say something like, "I can go from the door to the garage before the timer has emptied." See if the children's predictions are correct.

## *End:*

- Make a list of the things that you and the children were able to time during this activity.

## *Follow-up Activities:*

- Use a kitchen timer or stopwatch to time events for the children (for example, the children might pick up toys or put on their coats to go outdoors). Ask the children to predict how much time it will take to complete the tasks.

## 37. Noticing Changes in Nature

### Why This Is Important:

- The changes that take place in the natural cycles of plants and animals heighten children's awareness of the passage of time and the changes that occur.

### *Beginning:*

- Lay out the photos of the fruit tree on the table.
- Ask the children which photo is the first thing that happens before fruit can grow on a tree.

### *Middle:*

- Talk about each stage in the tree's cycle. For instance, the photos may show leaves; buds; flowers; small fruit; and, finally, ripe fruit. The photos may also show the tree after the fruit has been harvested, with leaves that change color and fall off.
- Encourage the children to talk about the photos and to put them in order.
- Go outside, and look at the trees with the children. Talk about the kinds of trees that you see. Ask "Do any of the trees bear fruit?"

### *End:*

- Find a deciduous tree (a tree that sheds its leaves for part of the year), and take a photo of the children in front of the tree.

### *Follow-up Activities:*

- Be sure to take pictures of the children in front of the tree during each season to notice the changes in the tree (and in the children)!

**CONTENT AREAS**
Science and Technology

**MATERIALS**

- Camera
- 8 photos illustrating the cycle of a fruit tree (or a tree appropriate for your geographic region)

- With the children, look at a family photo album that shows a child's growth from a baby to a preschooler or photos of a pet's growth from a puppy to dog or kitten to cat.

*A visit to a local fruit orchard gives the children a hands-on experience (and taste) of the stages in a tree's cycle.*

# Social Studies

**CONTENT AREAS**
Social Studies
Creative Arts

**MATERIALS**
- Blanket or flat sheet
- Paper plates, cups, and napkins
- Thermos and/or other items used on picnics
- Picnic basket or bag for carrying materials
- Dress-up items, such as hats or dolls

# 38. Going on a Picnic

## Why This Is Important:

- When children pretend, they imitate what they understand about the world and use their imaginations to express fantasies.
- Watching children's pretend play gives adults an opportunity to see how children picture the world.
- Adults can support children's pretend play by imitating what they are doing and letting them be the leaders of their play.

## Beginning:

- Ask the children if they have ever been on a picnic and, if so, what they remember about it.
- Explain that you would like to go on a picnic inside the house.

## Middle:

- Ask the children to help you figure out a good place to spread out the blanket.
- Invite the children to join you on the blanket for the picnic and to look through the basket with you.
- Ask the children what they would like to eat and drink.
- Continue the picnic, following the children's ideas about how the picnic should progress.

## End:

- Say that you must finish eating because it is getting late (or dark or because it looks like rain).
- Pack up the picnic, and pretend to go home.

## Follow-up Activities:

- Plan to eat a snack or meal outside on a blanket with the children.

Social Studies

# 39. Singing Songs

## Why This Is Important:

- Children enjoy exploring the wide range of sounds they can make with their voices, including humming and singing.
- Adults can sing along with children to encourage their singing and listen to a variety of musical styles.

### *Beginning:*

- Show the children the song cards, and see which songs they remember from your family child care home.

### *Middle:*

- Have the children choose several songs, and sing one together. Tap a steady beat on your legs before you begin singing.
- Ask the children if they know another song that is not on the song card. Encourage them to sing it for you. Using a blank card, add the name of the song as well as a symbol for the song so it can be added to the song book.

### *End:*

- Make up a song to let the children know it is time to move onto the next activity (use a familiar tune or make up your own tune). For example, sing the following words to the tune of "Here We Go 'Round the Mulberry Bush":

    Now it's time to go outside
    Go outside
    Go outside
    Now it's time to go outside
    I'll see you at the door.

### *Follow-up Activities:*

- Use blank cards to make new song cards with the children as their repertoire of songs grows.
- Think of different times of the day when you can use the song cards (for example, at snacktime).

**CONTENT AREAS**
Social Studies
Creative Arts

**MATERIALS**

- Song cards, each with the name of a familiar song and a simple picture or symbol to represent the song
- Blank cards

*A song book provides a visual reminder of the children's favorite songs in pictures and words.*

**CONTENT AREAS**
Social Studies
Creative Arts

**MATERIALS**
- Baby doll for each child
- Blankets
- Blank paper book

# 40. Babysitting

## Why This Is Important:

- Young children are developing skills to look at things from another person's point of view. They are also developing empathy.

- Giving children experiences in which they have opportunities to understand and practice caring for others leads to feelings of empathy.

## Beginning:

- Ask the children what they know about babies. Ask "What do babies need?"
- Give each child a baby doll.

## Middle:

- Talk about the children's suggestions for what a baby needs.
- See if there are items in your home that the children have suggested that a baby might need, such as a baby blanket or a small spoon for feeding.
- Let the children lead in caring for the babies.

## End:

- Sing a lullaby, such as "Rock-a-Bye Baby."
- Tell the children that there is a blank book to fill in about how the children "babysat" for their babies. Write down how the children cared for the baby. You might ask the children some or all of the following: "What did the baby eat?" "Where did the baby sleep?" "How did you play with the baby?"

## Follow-up Activities:

- Use an old baby bathtub or bucket to wash the dolls and doll clothes.

# About the Authors

**Suzanne Gainsley** is a HighScope certified trainer and teacher who has been teaching at the HighScope Demonstration Preschool since 1998. She has also worked with infants, toddlers, preschoolers, and elementary school children in various settings as a teacher, parent, and volunteer. Gainsley is the author of *From Message to Meaning: Using a Daily Message Board in the Preschool Classroom;* coauthor of two books in the Teacher's Idea Book Series (from HighScope Press), including *"I'm Older Than You. I'm Five!" Math in the Preschool Classroom* and *50 Large-Group Activities for Active Learners;* coauthor of *Activities for Home Visits: Partnering With Preschool Families;* and a contributing writer for *Small-Group Times to Scaffold Early Learning,* also in the Teacher's Idea Book Series.

**Julie Hoelscher** is an Early Childhood Specialist at the HighScope Educational Research Foundation. She has been an infant/toddler caregiver, preschool teacher, early childhood center director, resource counselor, teacher trainer, and an elementary school reform coach. Hoelscher is coauthor of *Activities for Home Visits* and also writes articles on classroom teaching practices for HighScope's *Extensions*.